PASSIVE INCOME

THE KEY TO FINANCIAL FREEDOM 2

TRADING, REAL ESTATE INVESTMENT AND INFOMARKETING

Table of Contents

REAL ESTATE INVESTMENT

SECTION ONE

INTRODUCTION TO REAL ESTATE INVESTMENT

Almost every working-class adult always dreams about that they don't have to do what they do for a living and yet their cash flow isn't disturbed. No one wants to remain stuck with their 9 to 5 jobs. Everyone wishes to spend time with their families, but we all know it is impossible because it does not meet modern-day lifestyle requirements. But what if there was away? What if it was possible to achieve financial freedom without having to work hard or not even work at all? Several ways can help you gain economic liberty, but the safest and most secure method is investing in real estate. Real estate investment is considered to be the key to live the luxurious life one always dreams of and in this article we are going to tell you how you can do that by putting your money to the right places.

Investing in real estate is a process often overlooked by persons who believe that it requires large sums of money and expert knowledge to get started. Wholesaling real estate is a viable real estate investment activity that provides new investors with the opportunity to get involved with limited funds and experience. Additionally, with the state of the current economy, many people are no longer able to afford their home due to various situations, including job loss, divorce, and even relocation. These create an excellent opportunity for wholesaling.

There are many reasons why real estate investment can fulfill all your dreams. They are as follows:

Capital Gains

You can get potential capital gains by investing in real estate properties. Real estate market tends to move upwards more than downwards, which is why there are good chances that you will make a considerable profit over your investment. For example, if you put $60,000 in a property and that property's value goes up by $20,000, that $20,000 will be your profit which you earned by just sitting at your home. Capital gains are often unrealized until the property is sold because that's when you know how much profit did you make, and those capital gains can also be used to invest in other features as well.

Online Investment

Development of online platforms has real estate investment opportunities at a distance of a few clicks. Crowdfunding platforms have been established, allowing almost everyone to invest in this industry and get profitable returns. Invest in real estate with only a few thousand dollars, and your investment can become worthy of millions in just a matter of days. Digital currencies have been developed through which payment methods have become online. Digital wallets are set up, and payments are transferred to the respective properties from one account to another.

Experienced Investors

If you are a newcomer and have money to invest but don't know your ways around the market, you should seek help from experienced real estate investors. The people who have undergone enough investment losses and market downturns can correctly guide you throughout your real estate investment journey. They can teach you how to invest efficiently and what kind of opportunities may produce profitable results for you. Those are the people who have successfully survived the dangerous setbacks and can also help you avoid them with their expertise.

Investing in Stable Markets

Before stepping into the real estate industry, you should make sure to avoid investing in the markets with high entry costs. Because if your resources are limited and that market happens to fall, you may not only lose your investment but might also go under a huge debt which often becomes very hard to lift off. Always look for the markets that are entirely in your range, and you don't have to suffer much in case the market takes a downturn.

WHY BE A REAL ESTATE INVESTOR

Here is a list of what I think are the advantages of being a real estate investor.

1. You write your own paycheck-95% of people that I know have to work harder in order to make more

money, I only need to work smarter. I know that a lot of people like the satisfaction of knowing that if they work x amount of hours they will get Y amount of pay. I realize that many people would real estate investing stressful, I would find it far more stressful to be at a 9 to 5 knowing that in order to make more money I would have to work more hours.

For example, I just closed a home Friday that I made a $17,000 net profit, That would be the equivalent to working the full year 2000 hours at $8.50 an hour, which a lot of people do. I had about 10-15 hours into the deal. My guys had to work hard, but I only had to write checks.

2. Knowing that if I fail, it's my darn fault-- Many people might see this as the considerable disadvantage of real estate, but I see it as one of the largest plusses.

In the era of corporate downsizing and very minimal job security, I cannot think of a boss in the whole world, then me. 99% of all jobs are there to make someone

else productive besides you. When you are a real estate investor, your only job is to make yourself productive.

I love knowing that if I do good, my paycheck will do good. If I do wrong, then my paychecks are bad. Its not like most jobs where there seems to be a large filter between both ends. With real estate investing if I put right in, I get good out, with most jobs you can put right, or even great in, yet you are dependent on what the human filter between you and the end.

Any hard worker who has been downsized will tell you that.

3. Freedom-Though real estate investing is not the big ball of freedom that many think it is. Many times you go from having one stupid boss to many stupid bosses. Essentially the housing inspectors, building inspectors, buyers, and sellers become your boss.

   The real freedom to me is waking up at 8-9 sitting with my family till 11, then going and looking at a couple of houses, if they look good then I sell them, or buy them, then go home. In the summer, I can drive my Corvette or Harley to look at homes, then head back and sit with my family by the pool.

4. No salary cap or timed raises-I had a friend of mine the other week telling me that she just got a raise of a Nickel and hour. What the heck does that equate to? Yeah, $2.00 a week. I have another friend who is engineers, and they reach their potential at $75,000.

Which is not bad money but, who would ever want to reach their potential, the sky is the limit in real estate. There are far more real estate millionaires that started with nothing, than corporate millionaires that started with nothing.

I like that you do not need a college education, you do not need to have the highest GPA, you can make it in real estate if wolves raised you under the shed in the back yard. Real estate does not have a glass ceiling or some stuffy corporate ladder. It does not involve having to kiss the rear of some boss who you loathe, to get a raise.

TIPS FOR GETTING STARTED IN REAL ESTATE INVESTMENT

Everything in this chapter is tools that can be applied to helping anyone get started in real estate investing. I am going to give you my eight keys to getting started. Nothing is right or wrong but reflects the point of view of the author. Laws and legal practices vary from state to state, and rules can change over time. The author does not vouch for the legality of his opinions, nor is there any intent to supply legal advice. The author strongly encourages the reader to consult with professionals and an attorney before entering in any real estate transaction or contract.

Let's get started on a fantastic adventure. The Tips are as follows:

- Desire
- Goal Setting

- Learning What To Do

- Attending a Real Estate Investing Seminar

- The Billings Montana Market

- Finding a Mentor

- Your Real Estate Team

- Just Do IT

1. Desire

Before we get into the bolts and nails of real estate investing, I want to talk to you about passion. If you are going to be successful at anything in life, including real estate investing, you have to have the desire to do it. Passion is defined as longing or craving, as for something that brings satisfaction or enjoyment. Desire stresses the strength of feeling and often implies firm intention or aim. In real estate investing if you don't have a desire to learn and grow as a human being and get satisfaction out of it, then real estate investing is going to be hard to do. When I go out and look at a property, it brings me a lot of enjoyment. Every aspect brings me joy from talking to homeowners, figuring out how I can make a deal work, to buying the house and to finding a good homeowner or tenant for the home. Real estate investing may not be for everyone, but real estate investing can offer anyone the financial freedom we all crave for. If you do not have the desire for real estate investing that is ok, it can still help you to live your dreams and help you to get where you want to go in the future.

Why is real estate investing a fantastic avenue for anyone to live out all of their dreams? Let me ask you a few questions. Do you have enough money to do anything you want? Do you have everything you want? No debt? A nice house? Great Marriage? The freedom to do anything regardless of how much it costs and the time it takes? If you have all of these things, then you are one of the few people in America who does. Most people may be working fifty hours a week and making just enough to pay their bills. In today's day and age, most people are living paycheck to paycheck never really knowing if they will make enough to pay the bills that keep piling up. If you cannot keep up with your monthly bills, how are you going to plan for retirement or send your kids to college or have time to enjoy life. The answer to all of these questions is becoming financially free. Now it's not going to be easy everyone will have to get off the couch and out of their comfort zone. Real estate is proven to be one of the fastest ways to get your out of the rat race of the nine to five and begin living the life you deserve to live. Everyone wants something different out of their life. Some dream of traveling the world, spending more time with family, volunteering, golfing, laying on a beach, giving back to the community, or anything that will make them happy. There are thousands of things that make people happy.

Making it in real estate takes a person who has a strong desire to change their lives for the better and think big. Anyone can become a great real estate investor. It is going to take a lot of work and can be a struggle at times, but in the end, it will be the most fantastic feeling ever. The people that make it in real estate investing all have a few things in common. First, they run their real estate investing business like any other business out there. Second, they get out there and network with anyone and everyone. Some people might be like me and have a hard time talking to other people. If you are that is ok, anyone can learn how to become a people person; it just takes hard daily work. You have to push yourself past your comfort zone. The third thing is that you cannot be afraid to fail. Everyone has failed at something, but the most successful people out their learn from their failures. The fourth thing is that you have to put a good team together. I will go into putting a team together in a later chapter. The concept of putting a team together is so that when you don't know something, you have team members that know what to do and can help you with questions. They can also make sure that you are not working yourself to death. You do not want to be the person doing everything in your business. Doing everything is a receipt for failure. You have to put together good people who you can trust and rely on. The fifth thing is that you need a mentor. Sixth and final is the desire to do it. No one can become successful at something if they don't want to do it and don't get satisfaction out of what they are doing.

2. Setting Goals

Having goals is one of the most critical aspects of achieving what you want in life. You don't want to have your goals up in your head you want to write them down and past what you have written on the wall somewhere or in the bathroom mirror. You want to review your goals daily and read them out loud to yourself. This way, you remind yourself every day why you are building your business.

How should you start to write down your goals? First, off you should think big, and by big, I mean HUGE. If your goals are too small, you will quickly achieve them and have nothing else to look forward also. You should start by asking yourself the question if I had all the money and time in the world what would I do, what would I buy, how would I spend my time, and how would I spend my energy. Are you starting to write these down? Well, you should be. Think about what you want, spending time with family, traveling the world, the best cars, a castle, owning a small country, running for president, having the most significant real estate investing business in your area or the state. Whatever your dreams and what you want out of your life, write it down. Some of my goals are becoming free, traveling the world, having a Ferrari, having ten vacation homes all over the world. Right now, I am just trying to get you out of your comfort zone of thinking and let your imagination run.

There are several ways to set goals. I have learned a lot of ways you can set your goals, and there is no right or wrong way. The best ways that I have found to set your goals is to break them up into two categories. First, your short term goals. This should be goals from a month out to around a year. The second is your long term goals; these goals are you think big goals and what you see for your future.

For year one, I like first to make a list of what I want to achieve this year, and I will give you an example of how to do that. For year one you want to be very specific first you want to list what you want your income to be at the end of the year, next how much cash in the bank you wish to (this is money in your checking account, not assets). Next, you want to list how much you are going to give. Giving is very important, this can be giving to charity, giving of gifts to friends and family, giving to your school or anything you can dream of. As long as what you give brings joy to others who need it more than you. Following list of what bad habits you have that you want to eliminate. Weather is quitting smoking, spending too much on junk, drinking too much, working too much, not spending enough time with family, too much TV, not exercising and many more. We all have bad habits that need to be changed for us to grow as human beings. Under each of these bad habits list out some steps that you can take to quit them. If your bad habit is being lazy and not exercising enough, what can you do to change that? Well, you can get a gym membership or a home work out program. Commit yourself you following through with a plan to work out 3-5 days a week. For you to change these bad habits, you have to be committed and follow through with a detailed plan you set for yourself. After you have your policies in place, you should start listing several things you want to achieve or do in the next year. You can start a successful business, spend time with family, travel to 2-5 places and so on. Now under each of these, you should also write a detailed plan on what you need and what you need to do to achieve these goals. Finally, you should take all of this information you have a write-on page on what you see your life being over the next year. Doing this is a great exercise to know what you want out of life.

Goals Year One

This is what I am going To Do This Year

Income: $500,000

Cash: $100,000

Give: $20,000

Bad Habits that will be changed:

Sleeping

1. Go to bed at 11 p.m.

2. Use a timer and set it for 8 hours

3. Set the timer on the other side of the room

Buying things that you don't need:

1. Going out shopping less

2. If you have the urge to buy something, think to yourself is thing item going to help me to achieve my goals of becoming financially free?

3. Tell friends what you are doing, so they can help to stop you.

What I want to Achieve:

Start a successful Real Estate Investing Business: (you should write a detailed step by step plan of everything you need to achieve your goal)

Travel: Where do I want to visit?

1. Gators football game (what I need to do it, money, etc.)

And last your page about what you want to achieve using words like I will and only positive words.

For long term goals, you don't need to be as specific right now, but you should list them and under them list a few steps or smaller goals that need to be achieved before you can reach them. With the long term, goals always think big. Another good exercise for long term goals is to make a collage of your goals. Put pictures of the house you want on it, places you want to travel, a photo of your family, what income you want in or anything you can think of.

3. *Learn*

Knowledge builds confidence and destroys fear. If you are starting any business, you need to learn the ins and outs of that business. The best way I have found to learn about real estate investing is to read all about it. But once you know it you have to apply what you have learned. Learning and reading is just one step to take. There are thousands of books on the market about real estate investing, and everyone has something you can learn from. You don't just want to read real estate investing books though. You also want to fill yourself with motivational and leadership books. Every successful person that I know if a reader and they all spend at least thirty minutes a day reading something that will teach them about improving their business or helping themselves to become a better person. Some of the best books that I would recommend reading are listed below.

- Rich Dad Poor Dad by Robert Kiyosaki (read this first and also ready everything in the rick dad unfortunate dad series, great books to start with and will expand your mind)
- Be a Real Estate Millionaire by Dean Graziosi
- Flip your way to financial freedom by Preston Ely (this is an E-Book)
- Four-hour workweek by Timothy Ferriss
- The Attractor Factor
- Short Sale Pre-foreclosure Investing by Dwan Bent-Twyford and Sharon Sestrepo
- Keys to success, by Napoleon Hill
- Think and Grow Rich by Napoleon Hill
- How to win friends and influence people
- Any Book by John C. Maxwell (he has tons of amazing leadership books)
- Getting Started in Real Estate Day Trading by Larry Goins
- The E Myth by Michael Gerber

- How to be a quick turn real estate millionaire by Ron Legrand

- The Power of Full Engagement

- The It Factor

- Anything by Anthony Robins

There are tons more you can read, but these will give you a great start. You should also read books on negotiating, sales, motivation, and biographies on American business people.

I hope this list gives you the knowledge it has given me. If you learn and apply what you have learned from these books, there is no reason that you should not become very successful.

4. Attend a Real Estate Investing Seminar

Attending a Real Estate Investing Seminar can be one of the best places to learn about real estate investing from some very well known experts. Several seminars are going on all over the country every weekend. If you live in a big city, it will be straightforward to find one. If you live in a town like Billings Montana, you might need to travel a little way to find one. Now, most of the best meeting cost money to attend them. Some range from five hundred dollars for three days, and some can be up to $20,000. There are a few that I would recommend. Than Merrill is a great speaker to hear. I have learned a ton from him. You can find his company online by Google searching for him. Also, rich dad poor dad has seminars all over the country. I attended one of their workshops in Billings Montana for only 500 dollars and learned a ton from it. There is also Preston Ely, Larry Goins, and hundreds of speakers out there. If you find a great book that you enjoyed, then just a simple search for that person online and see if they are speaking somewhere or offer a seminar close to you.

Another reason I recommend going to a seminar is that they get you pumped up and motivated. I have not yet found anything else that gets you feeling like you can do anything. When you get back from one of these seminars, you will have tons of energy and knowledge. Every time I get back from one, all I want to do is going out and do a deal or ten.

These seminars will also provide you with several opportunities to purchase amazing real estate investing tools, software, or learning material at a fraction of the cost. Believe me when I tell you all of the low priced seminars try to sell you something. But a lot of times what they are trying to sell is some excellent stuff.

Another reason to attend a seminar is to network with other investors and build relationships with them. You can meet other investors who you can partner with on a deal, sell a deal too, people who will provide you with deals and so on. You should have hundreds of business cards made up and try to give them all out. You never know how much one business card you hand out can make you.

5. Learn About the real estate market in your area

Most real estate investors start their career off my investing around where they live. This is why I do my real estate investing in Billings Montana. You can venture out when you have more experience. The reason behind this is because we feel more comfortable with the areas and know the neighborhoods better. It is also easier to get local real estate information that we need. Investing in your local market is also cheaper to start, there are fewer travel costs, you can see what you are buying, and it may give you a feeling a comfort.

First, you have to decide which part of town is the best place to invest in. This can be determined by what kind of real estate investing you choose to do. I have not gone over the types of real estate investing, but some include rehabbing (fixing up and selling), wholesaling (finding deals and selling them to other investors), buying to rent, and there are a few others. These are the real estate strategies that I use for the most part. When looking at the market, you need to see where other investors are buying their houses. Most of the best deals will be found in low to middle-class neighbors hoods. By little, I don't mean drug infested war zones, what I mean is blue collar safe neighborhoods that might have somewhat older houses and houses that are not on the higher end price side. Now you can find deals in the more top-priced communities, but most will be in the low to middle-income neighborhoods. When looking where others are buying, ask local realtors, other investors, or appraisers.

When talking with investors ask them several questions such as what neighborhoods they prefer, what type of houses they buy (3 bed two baths), and what they do (rehab, rent, wholesale). You should not look at other investors as competition but try and work with them.

There are different types of markets, such as appreciating markets, flat markets, and deprecating markets. Appreciating markets are markets that there is no enough houses or a very high demand for homes, which causes the price of houses to go up. The reason there is a high demand for housing can be because of job growth, a very appealing area, or several reasons. Flat markets are markets that have no or very little growth. This means that there is not a lot of demand; buy just enough to fill everyone's needs.

Depreciating markets are where there are a lot more houses than people to fill those house. This causes house prices to start going down. This can be because of a large employer leaving the area, a natural disaster, or just overbuilding. There is an old saying buy in a bust and sell in a boom. In depreciating markets, you can pick up several deals, while in appreciating the house prices are going to be much higher and harder to find great deals. The sale will still be out there you have to know where to find them.

Learning your market is another key to becoming successful. Real estate Brokers and experts in your area can be the best source of information for you. Learn to use them to find out what kind of market you are in. If you are in Billings, Montana, we are in a pretty stable market. Billings

Montana has not seen the ups and downs that other markets have experienced. I will have to say that I have been noticing a little bit of a downward trend but not much. Once the first time home buyer credit is over with we might see a bit of decline. Every market can vary by neighborhood, so make sure you know your market well. I have seen the same houses just one mile apart selling for totally different prices.

6. *Find a Mentor*

Having a mentor to help you can be your most significant learning experience. Mentors can help you with any questions you may have, walk you step by step through the investing process, give you moral support, you learn from their proven system, and also network you with others in the business. Every successful real estate investor that I know says they owe a lot of their success to the mentors they have and had in their lives. I have had one of the best mentors around my father. He is teaching me something new every day and pushing me to become successful.

When trying to find a mentor, I would suggest a network with the investors at your local real estate investors club meeting. There is a real estate investing club in Billings Montana that meets once a month. You can find information about real estate investing clubs in your area by searching for REA or real estate investors club then your area in Google. When you go to the meetings, ask around who the most prominent investors are. Then ask if you could get together with them sometime and discuss real estate investing. Ask them if they would consider working with you to get their career going. Offer your services as a bird dog. Bird dogs are people who go out find deals or leads about deals and give them to other investors. A bird dog gets from $500 to 3000 dollars depending on the agreement. Make sure that you have a bird dog contract signed with the investors saying that if you find them and deal and they buy it that you get paid a certain amount of money. Being a bird dog helps you to build credibility with the investor, and they are more likely to mentor you if you have something to offer them. If you would like to contact me with a question, go to my web site, Big Sky Property Solutions LLC.

7. Your Real Estate Team

Building a capable team can make your life as a real estate investor a lot easier. You are only one person and cannot do everything or be an expert in every aspect of real estate investing. Going to a project alone can become one of the most frustrating experiences you will ever encounter. Many people have become frustrated and quite real estate investing because they try and juggle too many things. Make sure that when putting a team together, you provide everyone with win-win opportunities.

When someone knows that working with you is going to make them money, they will put you as a higher priority on their list. But you have to prove it to them that you are the real deal.

People to have on your real estate investing team include

- Real Estate Agents (find the top agent for a volume of sales in your area and other agents who work with real estate investors)
- Real Estate appraisers (find an appraiser that has done a few hundred jobs or more and make sure they carry errors and omissions insurance)
- Real estate contractors (good rehab crews that can get the job done promptly have 3-5 teams and on every deal get three estimates done. Ask for referrals from them and make sure they are licensed)

- Real estate attorneys (every investor needs an attorney, they can help to protect your assets, make sure you find one that works with investors)
- A property management company (can manage your properties and will give you leads on the property they are achieving that might come up for sale)
- Title companies (take care of the legal process and make sure there are no liens against the property you are buying, choose one that does hundreds of closings a year)
- Home inspectors (charge about $400 but will give you an excellent inspection and could save you thousands in the long run)
- And your Mentor

All of these people can help you in various aspects of real estate investing. You might find that there are a couple of others that are keys to your business, but this is just a list of a few.

8. *Just Do it*

There is no better phrase out there then DO IT! Once you have learned all you can network with investors in Billings and learned real estate investing strategies, there is nothing left to do but get your feet wet. There is no better learning tool out there then doing a deal. Once you have completed that first deal, you will know what to expect and find out that it is not as hard as you thought it would be. You will have learned what you did right and what was frustrating. Take that experience and ask yourself what would have made it run smoother. Apply that to your next deal. Then the next sale will be more comfortable, and it keeps getting more relaxed as you go. I will say that every transaction is different from the last, but that what makes this business fun. You have to be creative and always keep on learning and growing with your business.

The average person never uses what they learn. Don't be average apply your knowledge. When going out and doing your first deal act like you have done 1000's of deals. The fastest way to change a habit is to act like it is true.

Five keys for success

1. Specialized Knowledge
2. Tools of a professional
3. Have the mindset of a winner
4. Mentors
5. Money and the knowledge of leveraging it (you don't have to have millions to invest in real estate, there are many strategies out there to use other people's money or no money at all)

HOW TO INVEST IN REAL ESTATE

Deciding how to invest in real estate means analyzing property types, strategies, potential risk, funding sources, average returns, and timelines. We'll review the most common ways to invest in real estate, including flipping houses, rental properties, buying vacation rental property, and purchasing commercial real estate. In other words, this is real estate investing 101.

4 Common Types of Real Estate Investing

Fix-and-Flips - Short-term investors who want to purchase, renovate, and sell a property.

Rental Property - Long-term investors, portfolio investors, and landlords who purchase real estate intending to build equity.

Vacation Rental Property - Investors who want to offset some of their vacation costs and build equity with rental income.

Commercial Real Estate - Business owners and experienced investors.

Here are four ways to get involved with real estate investing:

1. How to Invest in Real Estate Fix-&-Flips

Fix-and-flip investing is best for experienced, short-term investors wanting to purchase, renovate, and sell a property quickly. Flippers look for distressed properties with equity potential that can be flipped in 12 months or less for an average gross profit of 15% to 20%.

Who Fix-&-Flips Are Right For

Fix-and-flip real estate investing is best for real estate professionals such as real estate agents, brokers, and contractors, as well as experienced rehabbers. That's because flips, mainly leveraged deals, require careful selection of properties, targeted renovations, and efficient project execution for them to be lucrative. Novices risk low profits or potential losses when flipping.

As a rule of thumb, fix-and-flip real estate investing is best for investors with two to three or more past rehab projects. However, fix-and-flippers are sometimes inexperienced rehabbers who instead rely on licensed contractors to help them with renovations. When this is the case, the contractor provides the scope of the rehab work as well as a bid for the expected overall cost.

Fixing-and-flipping properties are the right real estate investment strategy if you have the following:

Experience: Most lenders will require previous experience in flipping properties. If you are new to fix-and-flip investing, hire, or partner with a contractor.

Time: Three or more months to devote to a fix-and-flip project; you need time to purchase, renovate, meet with contractors, monitor progress, and facilitate the sale.

Funds: Enough cash or credit to cover down payment requirements. You'll need at least 20% of a property's after repair value (ARV) in most cases.

Bargain Properties: Finding distressed properties before other investors and buying them below market value will be a crucial component of your success.

Team of Subcontractors: You will need to build relationships with contractors and subcontractors to ensure you get the best quality for the best price.

Contractors, real estate professionals, and investors who don't mind doing minor renovations themselves may be well suited for fix-and-flip real estate investing. For more information on investing in real estate through fix-and-flips, read our guide on how to make money flipping houses.

Costs of Fix-&-Flip Investing

There are four costs on a fix-and-flip investment: acquisition cost, renovations, holding costs, and sales cost. Subtracting these four expenses from a property's after repair value will allow you to estimate the profits on your flip. These costs should be carefully considered before purchasing a property to ensure your offer price leaves room for a respectable return.

Costs to anticipate in a fix-and-flip investment:

Acquisition Cost: Inspections ($350 to $700), earnest money deposits (1% to 2% of purchase price), lender application fees ($300 to $500), and closing costs.

Holding Costs: Interest-only mortgage payments, property taxes, utilities, and HOA fees. If monthly, multiply these cost by the time frame you expect to keep the property.

Renovation Cost: Depending on the scope of work, budget contractor cost, engineering, architects, demolition, building supplies, designers, and permitting fees.

Sales Cost: Real estate agent fees (5% to 6% of sales price) and seller closing costs (1% to 2%)

Managing fix-and-flip costs and timelines significantly impact your bottom line. Delays cost money; they should be expected and budgeted for when planning a fix-and-flip project, especially if you're new to flipping houses. If your investment is financed and delays arise, lenders may extend a loan's repayment terms for additional penalties and fees, but this further adds to the holding costs and reduces the net profit of any fix-and-flip investment.

Funding for Fix-&-Flip Real Estate Investments

Fix-and-flip investing is typically financed with short-term loans called hard money loans. These are interest-only loans that can be used to cover both the purchase and rehab of a flip. Hard money lenders generally lend up to 75% ARV with rates between 7.5% and 12%, fees of 1.5% to 2.5%, and repayment terms of three to 12 months.

Hard money loans are the most common type of fix-and-flip financing. But some investors pay for their fix-and-flip investments using all cash, often by using funds from a self-directed IRA. Cash allows investors to purchase houses quicker as compared to rehab loans, and also result in lower holding fees and closing costs, thus increasing an investor's potential profit.

Average Return of a Fix-&-Flip

The average gross return on a fix-and-flip is approximately 20%, calculated by taking the average fix-and-flip gross profit of $30,000 and dividing it by the average sale price of $150,000. The net return is the profit left after all expenses are paid. Yields will vary significantly based on the project and whether you've identified excellent properties to flip or not.

When reviewing your profits, budget for taxes on each fix-and-flip project. Profits for fix-and-flips are ideally earned within 12 months, creating a short-term capital gain and taxed at your ordinary-income bracket.

Potential Risks of Fix-&-Flips

While the reward is high, there are inherent risks in fix-and-flip real estate investing. If you're new and want to learn how to invest in real estate fix-and-flips, it's recommended that you work with a licensed contractor to gain experience managing rehab budgets and timelines. Overruns in cost and schedules are the most significant risk.

Correctly, fix-and-flip investors are exposed to:

- Higher-than-expected rehab costs: An investor may budget $10,000 to replace a roof, but once the old roof is removed, extensive rotten wood is found, adding value.
- Higher-than planned to hold costs: If a project takes longer than expected to complete, say two extra months, you'll need to subtract the value from your profit.

- Loan extension penalties: If your property doesn't sell as fast as you thought it would, your lender may extend the loan but will charge penalties that eat into your profit.

Average Investment Timeline for a Fix-&-Flip

The average timeline for a fix-and-flip project is six months. Hard money lender terms are typically around 12 months. The faster a rehab investor can sell a fixer-upper, the fewer monthly holding costs and the likelihood of penalties, thus increasing potential profit.

Processes that affect an investor's timeline:

Due diligence: Mechanical inspections and home inspections (10 business days)

Loan process: 15 to 30 days

Permitting: 10 to 30 days

Contractor availability: Depends on season and construction market

Real estate market: Buyer's market or seller's market

Closing time frame: 30 to 90 days

As investors gain experience flipping properties and assemble teams of contractors, real estate agents, and lenders they can rely on, they will increase efficiency and reduce this timeline. If the market's suitable, they may decide to make the most of that experience and productivity by starting a house-flipping business.

2. How to Invest in Rental Properties

Investing in rental properties (aka buy-and-hold real estate investing) is best for investors planning to own the real estate long term and plan to manage or outsource management. Buy-and-hold investors look for rental income, market appreciation, and tax benefits. Lenders offer rental owners rates starting at 5% with up to 30-year terms and 80% LTV.

Who Rental Property Investing Is Right For

Rental property investing is best for passive long-term investors looking to purchase a residential rental property, and it is a popular strategy for real estate beginners. Long-term rentals offer better financing options and lower equity requirements, making entry into these investments easier. These properties include single-family homes, apartment buildings, and multifamily units.

Typical forms of buy-and-hold investors:

Landlords: Own one to three rental properties and manage the properties themselves with the help of property management software.

Portfolio Investors: Own four to ten-plus rental properties and rely on property management companies.

Turnkey Investors: Investors who purchase properties away from their home with a tenant and management company in place.

Costs of Rental Property Investing

Costs associated with a buy-and-hold property are property maintenance, marketing for tenants, and managing the property. A good rule of thumb for estimating maintenance is 1.5 times the monthly rent per year, and management fees range from 8% of ongoing monthly gross rent to one full month's rent for new tenant signup.

Additional costs associated with a buy-and-hold real estate investment include:

Financing Costs: Loan origination fees and any points

Closing Costs: Generally 2% to 5% of the purchase price

Utilities: For common areas that the landlord is responsible for paying

Property Taxes: Taxes are typically higher for an investment property, approximately 2% of the value

Rental Property Insurance: Yearly average $1,473 to $1,596 on a $200,000 investment property

HOA Fees: If the property is a condo or part of a neighborhood HOA, fees can cover exterior maintenance, common area utilities, and amenities

Funding for Rental Property Investing

Buy-and-hold investors who are not paying cash rely on conventional mortgages to fund their investment purchases. Some buy-and-hold investors start as rehabbers, relying on hard money loans to renovate a property; once rented, they refinance to a conventional mortgage.

Terms of a conventional investment property loan can include:

Loan Amount: 80% – 96.5% of a house's purchase price

Interest Rates: 5.0% – 8.00%

Lender Fees: 0% – 1%

Terms: 15 years – 30 years

Average Return on Rental Property Investments

The average return on a buy-and-hold property is currently 9% ROI. This average takes into account the investment's annual net income and the annual equity build or loss from market appreciation or depreciation. This variable return is driven by the local real estate market, the property's ongoing expenses, and the property's vacancy rate.

An investor can increase returns by purchasing a property under market value. REO properties and foreclosures may offer higher equity opportunities. Also, keeping monthly expenses and the vacancy rate low ensures a stable cash flow. A vacancy rate of 5% is considered good, meaning the property is vacant only 5% of the year.

Potential Risks of Rental Property Investing

The risks to consider in buy-and-hold real estate investing are a low occupancy rate, damage to the property, increasing taxes and insurance, late pays and eviction rates, and price depreciation.

Ways to mitigate the potential risks of buy-and-hold investing:

- Keep high occupancy rates by pricing your rental correctly
- Keep on top of needed repairs by completing quarterly inspections
- Purchase proper landlord liability insurance to protect yourself from on-site injuries due to negligence or lack of care. Enforce strict procedures for tenant pre-screening, ensuring quality tenants.

Screen tenants: Late pays, evictions, and property damage can bring unwanted expenses. Enforce tenant screening with companies like MyRental.

Research before you purchases: Price depreciation is tied to the local market and is difficult to avoid. Research the neighborhood and buy-in stable or up-and-coming areas to reduce potential market risk.

Average Investment Timeline for Rental Properties

The holding time for a buy-and-hold investor is between five to 30-plus years. The benefit of holding a property for 30 years is the opportunity to capture long-term growth, build wealth through equity and property appreciation, and avoid short-term capital gains.

Keeping a buy-and-hold property until it reaches a specific value, say in five years, is another way to create wealth. This strategy relies on the real estate market to dictate timelines. When the market peaks, buy-and-hold investors will sell their properties, realize the gains, and get the cash ready for the next buyer's market cycle.

Where to Get Rental Property Financing

Getting a great mortgage for your rental property has never been easier. Fill out a short form on LendingTree and let multiple lenders compete for your loan. Their online marketplace enables you to quickly compare rates, offers, and find a good fit. Take a few minutes and see your options.

3. How to Invest in Real Estate with Vacation Rentals

Vacation rental property is a property an investor buys to use as a vacation home and also to rent out to offset the costs of ownership. It's typically purchased in an area that has tourist attractions and amenities. Most investors hire a management company to handle marketing, scheduling, upkeep, and rent collection. Conventional financing terms are available for most other home rentals.

Who Vacation Rental Property Is Right For

Investing in vacation rental property can be a good option for experienced investors and new investors alike. It's an excellent way for real estate beginners because you get the benefit of using the property yourself and renting it when you're not using it.

Vacation rental property benefits:

- A source of supplemental income that can offset home ownership and vacation costs
- Rental property tax deductions
- Real estate investing for beginners because it has lower down payment requirements than non-owner occupied loans
- Costs of a Vacation Rental Property

Typical costs of investing in a vacation rental property include:

Lender Fees: Loan origination fees and any lender points

Closing Costs: Generally 2% to 5% of the purchase price

Property Taxes: Varies depending on the size and location of the property

Vacation Rental Property Insurance: The average vacation rental insurance yearly premium is $2,000 to $3,000

Maintenance and Cleaning: Varies, but averages 1% to 2% of the property's purchase price per year

Property Management Fees: Typically 15% to 30% of the rent

Vacation rental property typically generates higher rents than a buy-and-hold real estate investment, but the costs such as insurance, cleaning, and maintenance are generally higher too.

Funding for a Vacation Rental Property

- Investors typically fund a vacation rental property with a conforming loan. Lenders will lend up to 90%

of the sales price to prime borrowers with up to 30-year terms and conforming loan rates.

- An investor may use a portfolio loan if they don't meet the personal qualifications for a conforming loan.

Multifamily Loan for Vacation Rental Property

An investor will generally use a multifamily loan to finance a vacation rental property with two to four units. There are four types of multifamily loans: conventional mortgages, government-backed loans, portfolio loans, and short-term multifamily financing. Each type of investment has its lending criteria.

For more specific information on multifamily loans, check out our in-depth multifamily loan guide, which includes things like where to find multifamily loans and how to apply for them.

Average Returns on Investing in Vacation Rental Property

Returns on a real estate vacation rental property vary based on the purchase price of the property, the location, operating expenses, and the occupancy rate. Typical returns on a vacation rental property are similar to a buy-and-hold investment and are usually around 9% to 12%.

Factors that affect your vacation property ROI are:

Management Fees: Average 28% for a vacation management company

Property Taxes: Typically 2%-plus of the assessed property value

Financing Costs: Interest rate, lender fees, and monthly mortgage payments

Operational Expenses: Cleaning costs, maintenance, etc.

HOA Fees: If applicable, these can vary based on unit size and amenities in the building

Occupancy Rates: The more the property is rented, the higher your ROI will be

Potential Risks of Investing in Vacation Rental Property

The significant risks in investing in vacation rental property are extended vacancies, not being able to carry the costs associated with the property, and hurricane damage if it is located near the beach.

Some risks of investing in a vacation rental property include:

- Inconsistent cash flow because renters are usually seasonal
- Carrying costs such as property taxes, maintenance, and utility bills, regardless of whether the property is rented or not

- Property management fees

- Vacation rental properties are hit harder during economic downturns because people often eliminate or cut back on vacations to save money

"Some risks associated with investing in vacation rental property are poor weather forecasts, spikes in gasoline prices, beach closings because of either a natural phenomenon or man-made, and unusual wear-and-tear on furniture."

– Chris Dowler, Founder & Owner, Dowler Construction Services

Average Timeline for Investing in Vacation Rental Property

Investors typically keep vacation rental properties for more than five years, making them a buy-and-hold investment strategy. Some investors keep these properties in the family for long-term wealth, while others sell when they can no longer enjoy them.

For more information on buying vacation rental property, check out our in-depth guide on how to buy a vacation rental property, which includes things like what to look for in a vacation rental property and what areas to buy-in.

Where to Get Vacation Rental Property Financing

Finding the right lender for your vacation rental property doesn't have to be a headache. Fill out a short form on LendingTree and let lenders compete for your business. Their online marketplace allows you to compare rates, offers quickly, and find a good fit. See your options online in minutes.

4. How to Invest in Commercial Real Estate

Commercial properties are purchased by investors and leased out to companies and include office spaces, restaurants, and retail stores. Commercial real estate investors are mostly long-term investors looking for monthly lease income and price appreciation. Commercial investors can use traditional long-term loans or commercial hard money lenders for fix-and-flips.

Who Commercial Real Estate Investing Is Right For

Commercial real estate investing is right for business owners who want to own the property their business is located on and for well-funded experienced investors. Commercial real estate can be more complicated and cash-intensive than investing in residential real estate. Most lenders require 20% to 25% down, and charge rates between 8% and 10%.

The most common types of commercial real estate investors include:

- Businesses and corporations seeking their own office spaces
- Real estate investment funds that invest in commercial-only or commercial+residential
- Limited partnerships that pool funds and diversify risk for smaller commercial investors
- Experienced individual investors with a higher tolerance for risk, access to funding, and familiarity with commercial real estate leases

Costs of Commercial Real Estate Investing

Commercial real estate is cash-intensive, lender rates are higher and less flexible, taxes are generally higher, and insurance is typically more expensive than residential. However, commercial property owners can pass many of these costs over to the tenant with a triple net lease.

Commercial real estate investment costs generally include:

Lender Fees and Closing Costs: Loan origination fees, any points the lender charges, and closing costs of 2% to 5% of the purchase price

Property Taxes: Generally higher than residential real estate investments, based on location and building size

Liability Insurance: Protects the owner from on-site liability

Utilities: Landlord may pay for common areas, and the tenant generally pays all other services

Some commercial real estate costs, such as property taxes, maintenance, and licenses, are usually paid in part or in full by the tenant as part of the terms of their lease.

Funding for a Commercial Real Estate Investment

Commercial mortgages are funded by traditional banks, SBA loans, and hard money loans with loan terms between 12 months and 25 years. Interest rates are fixed or variable, typically between 6% and 10%. Commercial loans require commercial appraisals, which are expensive, and some lenders have prepayment penalties.

Commercial loans come in four different types:

- Traditional commercial mortgage: 60% to 80% LTV, variable and fixed rates, and up to 25-year terms

- SBA 7(a) loan for commercial real estate: LTV up to 90%, $50,000 to $5 million, up to 25-year term, and variable rates

- CDC/SBA 504 loan for commercial real estate: Owner-occupied loan with LTV up to 90%, minimum $125,000 to $20 million, up to 25-year term, and fixed rates

- Hard money loans for commercial real estate: LTV up to 70%, 250,000 to $3 million, up to 12-month terms, and rates starting at 10%

For more information on the different commercial mortgage options, check out our article on the types of commercial real estate loans.

Commercial real estate investors also rely on hard money loans to fund their investment purchases. If a commercial real estate investor wants to renovate a property, either to sell or to lease out long term, they can use a hard money lender upfront and then a traditional lender for the long-term take-out mortgage.

Average Return on Commercial Real Estate Investing

The 20-year average return on commercial real estate is approximately 9.5% gross return on investment (ROI). Commercial real estate investors earn a return on monthly lease income as well as on price appreciation when they sell.

The return is gross and therefore, doesn't include any costs, such as:

- Monthly Loan Payments: Based on the purchase price and specific lender
- Commercial Property Taxes: Roughly 2% of the fair market value annually
- Repairs and Maintenance for Investor Managed Properties: Generally 2% of fair market value annually

- Property Management Fees for Commercial Portfolio Investors: Generally 15% to 35% of annual gross lease income

These expenses, similar to buy-and-hold residential investors, eat into the profits of a commercial real estate investor. Investors can increase their returns if they find a commercial real estate foreclosure or if they buy a property at auction.

Potential Risks of Commercial Real Estate Investing

Commercial real estate investors generally face the following risks:

Occupancy Risk: Risk of an empty property and tenants destroying the property (which takes time and money to repair), negatively affecting the ROI.

Lease Price Depreciation: The commercial real estate leasing market can dip lower than the borrower's mortgage, causing the investor to become "underwater."

Liability Risk: Owners can be held liable for on-site injuries due to negligence or lack of care. Commercial investors can protect themselves with commercial real estate liability insurance.

Average Investment Timeline for Commercial Real Estate Investing

The average investment timeline of a commercial real estate investment is more than five years. This is because the financing terms are typically between five years and 25 years, and many investors hold commercial real estate properties longer than the maximum financing term.

The average lease for a commercial real estate property is also between three years and five years. Commercial real estate investors, therefore, have longer-term tenants than the tenants of residential properties. This extends an investor's average investment timeline and makes commercial investors more likely to buy-and-hold.

Where to Get Commercial Real Estate Financing

You can find a commercial real estate loan at your bank, credit union, or through an online lender like RCN Capital. RCN Capital lends on commercial properties such as apartment buildings and mixed-use buildings while offering competitive rates to prime borrowers. You can apply online in just a few steps.

Alternative Real Estate Investing Options

There are several alternative ways of investing in real estate. These generally include real estate crowdfunding, investing in real estate investment trusts (REITs), and tax liens. Each of these alternative investments has its risks and rewards and are generally right for different kinds of investors.

Real estate crowdfunding companies provide opportunities to invest in loan-backed, single-family homes, apartments, condos, and multi-unit properties. REITs are corporations that own or finance income-producing real estate. They typically hold a portfolio of real estate within a specific sector and generally payout 90% of annual profits to investors.

The most popular alternative real estate investments are:

Investing in Real Estate Crowdfunding. Real estate crowdfunding pools money from multiple investors to fund a project or portfolio of projects. Real estate crowdfunding is right for passive accredited and non-accredited investors who want to invest in a project that would otherwise be out of their price range or geographic location.

Real estate crowdfunding websites use pools of accredited investors' cash to fund loans to various borrowers, and average returns of 6% to 10% for both short-term and long-term opportunities. LendingHome, for example, lists average returns for accredited crowdfunding investors at 7.25%. Returns from crowdfunding investments come as a portion of the interest rate charged to the borrower.

Since real estate crowdfunding investments are individual loans, there is the risk of the borrower not making their monthly payments and not being able to repay the loan in full when due. The real estate crowdfunding loan duration is typically one to five years.

Real Estate Investment Trust (REITs) Investments

REITs are corporations that own or finance income-producing properties. REITs give investors more liquidity and can be traded like stock without the investor acting as a landlord. They have a lower buy-in amount, so it's generally cheaper to invest in a REIT than to buy a property.

Other important details about how to invest in real estate REITs include:

Cash required: Investors in REITs put up their cash, like buying a stock or mutual fund.

No mortgage loan: Investors don't solely own the property, so you can't take out a mortgage loan on the properties.

Returns: Depending on the type of REIT, the average performance varies. You're generally investing less money than a purchased property requires, so returns are usually lower.

Control: You won't have control of the investment. A management team controls REITs, and they make all the decisions.

Less tax write-off: REITs have no depreciation write-offs.

Investment time: A private REIT requires investors to keep their investments in the REIT for at least one to two years.

REITs can be an excellent way to start investing in real estate if you have cash, want to diversify your real estate holdings, and don't want to manage projects or properties. For more information on REITs, read our in-depth guide to investing in REITs.

Tax Lien & Tax Deed Investing

Purchasing properties with tax liens is real estate investing where investors purchase properties with delinquent tax balances. Investors pay the delinquent tax and earn interest and fees on their investment. They're right for investors who have cash, want to earn interest and penalty income, and possibly acquire a property for below-market value.

The return on tax lien investments varies by state. Each municipality gives the delinquent homeowner a redemption period. This is the time the owner has to pay their tax balance in full plus penalties and interest, and that time can be months or years. For more information, check out our guide to tax deed investing.

Bottom Line: Real Estate Investing 101

Real estate investing can offer income and equity opportunities, diversification, and tax benefits. The most common investments are a rental property, vacation rentals, fix-and-flip projects, and commercial real estate. However, investing in REITs, crowdfunding, and tax liens can also be good options. As with all investments, the right choice for you will depend on the size of the investment you're looking to make, the return you expect, and the amount of risk you're comfortable with.

TRADING

SECTION TWO

INTRODUCTION TO TRADING

Financial freedom means different things to different people. But, at its core, it is about the ability to make choices that you otherwise would not be able to make. Haven't you heard that old age-old question, "What would you do if you had a million dollars?" Granted, the amount hasn't increased since the theoretical question was first invented. We might be better off asking what one would do if they had ten million dollars, but you get the point. It's supposed to illustrate to use what we truly love doing, that is, if money was of no concern. If funds and expenses were of no consequence to you, would you still have the same job or career that you do now? While I am sure, there are some cases of people who would say yes, I know many others that would most definitely say no. How do you gain the freedom to say no to work you don't want to do and yes to the life experiences that matter to you? It is simple: You spend way less than you earn.

Now, there are a couple of ways you can do that. You can cut your spending way down, to subsist at a level that allows you to save and invest conservatively while still making that paltry salary the tedious cubicle job affords you. Our you could up your skills and earn way more than you spend, by creating a second stream of income, eventually building up that stream of income to eclipse the first, paltry stream. Multiple income streams are a must for anyone eyeing early retirement. You need to protect yourself for downturns in the stock market, housing values, sales commissions, or any other type of investment or revenue stream you currently enjoy.

One of the best ways to create that second stream of income is to become a day trader. You can make money off stocks that move up and down during the trading day, but you need to have a coherent strategy, rock-solid risk management instincts, and a willingness to study and do research. There are day trading education sites out there that can teach you the procedure and give you a chance to hone your skills in trading chat rooms with veteran day traders and trading simulators.

Now, it needs to be said that day trading is not a way to get rich quickly. You need to learn your way to competence before you can begin to make even small profits. But that can be a stepping stone to bigger and better things. As with all investments, there is an inherent risk, so you should only invest in the level that you are comfortable and can afford the cyclical nature of the markets. Investing, and specifically, day trading takes a certain amount of time and discipline to master and get good at.

Veteran day traders can take a small amount of money and build it back up into a real severe pile of cash. After years of learning the market, they can take a couple of months to trade their way to six figures, faster than noobs on the market. That's why it pays to stick with it even if you hit a rough patch or two to start.

Key messages and adages:

- Get around real traders if you are serious about trading. People who trade for a living, those are the people you need around you. They have the skill, habits, and experience in selling and that will rub off on you

- It's all about statistics, probability, and patterns – I can already hear you going "foul" you saying that because you are a mathematician. Not really. Forex Trading uses a lot of mathematics, but you don't need maths to be good at it. Mathematics is an added advantage

- When you chose to work – remember that you want to exchange your time for money.

- Always make sure you have the second source of income in place – makes an example of a comfortable life he lived as a middle class while his father went up to the corporate ladder in the retail sector but soon went bankrupt during the recession and his parents divorced due to financial complications

- Consistency and commitment are essential elements in trading

- There is a different type of traders, those who trade in the morning before work and after work, and there are those who trade from 6 am to 6 pm. If you are in a full-time job better trade in the morning and evening so that you won't have to trade under your office table. I loved this point

- 20% of traders will succeed, and 80% will fail

- Learn to handle your emotions. If you win, don't put your shirt over your head in celebration. If you lose, don't throw your computer screen against the wall. Learn to manage your emotions. That is important for trading

- Real traders must show you the amount of money they make and also the amount of money lost. If a trader does not show you what they lost, there is something they are hiding. Remember, you can still make more losses and even make money.

UNDERSTANDING THE DIFFERENT WAYS TO BUY AND SELL STOCK

The following are general descriptions of some of the common order types and trading instructions that investors may use to buy and sell stocks. Please note that some of the order types and trading instructions described below may not be available through all brokerage firms. Furthermore, some brokerage firms may offer additional order types and trading instructions not described below.

Investors should contact their brokerage firms to determine which types of orders and trading instructions are available for buying and selling as well the firms' specific policies regarding such available rules and trading instructions. Market and Limit Orders The two most common order types are the market order and the limit order. Market Order A market order is an order to buy or sell a stock at the best available price.

Generally, this type of law will be executed immediately. However, the rate at which a market order will be completed is not guaranteed. Investors need to remember that the last traded price is not necessarily the price at which a market order will be executed. In fast-moving markets, the rate at which a market order will perform often deviates from the last-traded price or "real-time" quote. Example: An investor places a market order to buy 1000 shares of XYZ stock when the best offer price is $3.00 per share. If other orders are executed first, the investor's market order may be completed at a higher price. Besides, a fast-moving market may cause parts of a large market order to execute at different rates.

Example: An investor places a market order to buy 1000 shares of XYZ stock at $3.00 per share. In a fast-moving market, 500 shares of the Order could execute at $3.00 per share, and the other 500 shares perform at a higher price. Limit Order A limit order is an order to buy or sell a stock at a specific price or better. A buy limit order can only be executed at the limit price or lower, and a sell limit order can only be completed at the limit price or higher. A limit order is not guaranteed to execute. A limit order can only be filled if the stock's market price reaches the limit price. While limit orders do not guarantee execution, they help ensure that an investor does not pay more than a predetermined price for a stock.

Example: An investor wants to purchase shares of ABC stock for no more than $10. The investor could place a limit order for this amount that will only execute if the price of ABC stock is $10 or lower. Special Orders and Trading

Instructions In addition to market and limit orders, brokerage firms may allow investors to use special orders and trading instructions to buy and sell stocks. The following are descriptions of some of the most common special orders and trading instructions. Stop Order A stop order, also referred to as a stop-loss order, is an order to buy or sell a stock once the price of the stock reaches a specified price, known as the stop price. When the stop price is reached, a stop order becomes a market order. A buy stop order is entered at a stop price above the current market price. Investors generally use a buy stop order to limit a loss or to protect a profit on a stock that they have sold short. A sell stop order is entered at a stop price below the current market price. Investors generally use a sell stop order to limit a loss or to protect a profit on a stock that they own. Before using a stop order, investors should consider the following: n short-term market fluctuations in a stock's price can activate a stop order, so a stop price should be selected carefully. n The stop price is not the guaranteed execution price for a stop order. The stop price is a trigger that causes the stop order to become a market order. The execution price an investor receives for this market order can deviate significantly from the stop price in a fast-moving market where prices change rapidly. An investor can avoid the risk of a stop order executing at an unexpected price by placing a stop-limit order, but the limit price may prevent the Order from being executed. For certain types of stocks, some brokerage firms have different standards for determining whether a stop price has been reached. For these stocks, some brokerage firms use only last-sale prices to trigger a stop order, while other firms use quotation prices. Investors should check with their brokerage firms to determine the specific rules that will apply to stop orders. Stop-limit Order A stop-limit order is an order to buy or sell a stock that combines the features of a stop order and a limit order. once the stop price is reached, a stop-limit order becomes a limit order that will be executed at a specified price (or better). The benefit of a stop-limit order is that the investor can control the price at which the Order can be executed. Before using a stop-limit order, investors should consider the following: As with all limit orders, a stop-limit order may not be executed if the stock's price moves away from the specified limit price, which may occur in a fast-moving market. n short-term market fluctuations in a stock's price can activate a stop-limit order, so stop and limit prices should be selected carefully. The stop price and the limit price for a stop-limit order do not have to be the same.

For example, a sell stop limit order with a stop price of $3.00 may have a limit price of $2.50. such an order will become an active limit order if market prices reach $3.00, although the Order could only be executed for $2.50 or better.

For certain types of stocks, some brokerage firms have different standards for determining whether the stop price of a stop-limit order has been reached. For these stocks, some brokerage firms use only last-sale prices to trigger a stop-limit order, while other firms use quotation prices. Investors should check with their brokerage firms to determine the specific rules that will apply to stop-limit orders.

Day Orders, Good-Til-Cancelled Orders, and Immediate-Or-Cancel Orders Day orders, Good-til-Cancelled (GtC) orders, and Immediate-or-Cancel (IoC) orders represent timing instructions for an order and may be applied to either market or limit orders. unless an investor specifies a time frame for the expiration of an order, orders to buy and sell a stock are Day orders, meaning they are good only during that trading day. A GTC order is an order to buy or sell a stock that lasts until the Order is completed or canceled. Brokerage firms typically limit the length of time an investor can leave a GtC order open. This time frame may vary from broker to broker. Investors should contact their brokerage firms to determine what time limit would apply to GtC orders. An IOC order is an order to buy or sell a stock that must be executed immediately. Any portion of the Order that cannot be filled immediately will be canceled. Fill-Or-Kill and All-Or-None Orders two other common special order types are Fill-Or-Kill (FOK) and All-Or-None (AON) orders. An FoK order is an order to buy or sell a stock that must be executed immediately in its entirety; otherwise, the entire Order will be canceled (i.e., no partial execution of the Order is allowed). An Aon order is an order to buy or sell a stock that must be executed in its entirety, or not executed at all. However, unlike the FoK orders, Aon orders that cannot be executed immediately remain active until they are executed or canceled.

Opening Transactions Investors should be aware that any order placed outside of regular trading hours and designated for trading only during regular hours will usually be eligible to execute at an opening price. Investors should contact their brokerage firms to find out their broker's policies regarding opening transactions.

TWO STEPS THAT WILL PUT YOU AHEAD OF THE CROWD

The two critical skills that separate winners from losers are risk control and self-control. Managing risk in your account is pretty straightforward once you know the formulae, which you're about to see. A professional trader may allocate up to a third of his research time to calculating money management angles, as he compares risks and rewards for different stocks. He discards many stocks that look attractive but whose risk parameters don't suit him. How much time does an average beginner spend calculating and managing risk? Most likely zero, zip, nada.

Right before placing a trade he may briefly scratch his head or some other part of his anatomy and decide to double his usual size because he made money in the previous business or skip this trade because he lost money in his last trade.

Both choices are equally wrong. If you let your latest trade determine what size to trade next time, it means giving up control of trade management. If you follow the formulae in this book for controlling risks, you'll accomplish a goal in which most beginners fail.

The second essential skill – self-control – is harder to quantify. Fortunately, there is a clear and concrete tool for implementing and measuring self-control: keeping good quality trading records.

HOW TO CONTROL RISK

An intelligent scuba diver always keeps an eye on his air tank's pressure gauge to make sure he has enough to return to the surface, with a safety margin. The money in your trading account is your air supply. Watch it, be economical in its use, and have a reserve. All beginners, no matter how bright, make mistakes, and take losses. Be sure to keep your losses small, don't let them threaten your survival.

Risk management helps cut down losses. It can also help protect a trader's account from losing all of his or her money. The risk occurs when the trader suffers a loss. If it can be managed, the trader can open him or herself up to making money in the market.

It is an essential but often overlooked prerequisite to successful active trading. After all, a trader who has generated substantial profits can lose it all in just one or two bad trades without a proper risk management strategy. So how do you develop the best techniques to curb the risks of the market?

KEY TAKEAWAYS

- Trading can be exciting and even profitable if you can stay focused, do due diligence, and keep emotions at bay.

- Still, the best traders need to incorporate risk management practices to prevent losses from getting out of control.

- Having a strategic and objective approach to cutting losses through stop orders, profit-taking, and protective puts is a smart way to stay in the game.

Planning Your Trades

As Chinese military general Sun Tzu's famously said: "Every battle is won before it is fought." This phrase implies that planning and strategy – not the battles – win wars. Similarly, successful traders commonly quote the phrase: "Plan the trade and trade the plan." Just like in war, planning can often mean the difference between success and failure.

First, make sure your broker is right for frequent trading. Some brokers cater to customers who trade infrequently. They charge high commissions and don't offer the right analytical tools for active traders.

Stop-loss (S/L) and take-profit (T/P) points represent two key ways in which traders can plan when trading. Successful traders know what price they are willing to pay, and at what price they are ready to sell. They can then measure the resulting returns against the probability of the stock hitting their goals. If the adjusted performance is high enough, they execute the trade.

Conversely, unsuccessful traders often enter a trade without having any idea of the points at which they will sell at a profit or a loss. Like gamblers on a lucky — or unlucky streak — emotions begin to take over and dictate their trades. Losses often provoke people to hold on and hope to make their money back, while profits can entice traders to hold on for even more gains imprudently.

Consider the One-Percent Rule

A lot of day traders follow what's called the one-percent rule. This rule of thumb suggests that you should never put more than 1% of your capital or your trading account into a single trade. So if you have $10,000 in your trading account, your position in any given instrument shouldn't be more than $100.

This strategy is common for traders who have accounts of less than $100,000 — some even go as high as 2% if they can afford it. Many traders whose accounts have higher balances may choose to go with a lower percentage. That's because as the size of your account increases, so too does the position. The best way to keep your losses in check is to keep the rule below 2% — any more, and you'd be risking a substantial amount of your trading account.

Setting Stop-Loss and Take-Profit Points

A stop-loss point is a price at which a trader will sell a stock and take a loss on the trade. This often happens when a trade does not pan out the way a trader hoped. The points are designed to prevent the "it will come back" mentality and limit losses before they escalate. For example, if a stock breaks below a critical support level, traders often sell as soon as possible.

On the other hand, a take-profit point is a price at which a trader will sell a stock and make a profit on the trade. This is when the additional upside is limited, given the risks. For example, if a stock is approaching a critical resistance level after a significant move upward, traders may want to sell before a period of consolidation takes place.

How to More Effectively Set Stop-Loss Points

Setting stop-loss and take-profit points are often done using technical analysis, but fundamental analysis can also play a key role in timing. For example, if a trader is holding a stock ahead of earnings as excitement builds, he or she may want to sell before the news hits the market if expectations have become too high, regardless of whether the take-profit price has been hit.

Moving averages represent the most popular way to set these points, as they are easy to calculate and widely tracked by the market. Key moving averages include the 5-, 9-, 20-, 50-, 100- and 200-day averages. These are best set by applying them to a stock's chart and determining whether the stock price has reacted to them in the past as either a support or resistance level.

Another great way to place stop-loss or take-profit levels is on support or resistance trend lines. These can be drawn by connecting previous highs or lows that occurred on significant, above-average volume. Like with moving averages, the key is determining levels at which the price reacts to the trend lines and, of course, on high volume.

When setting these points, here are some key considerations:

- Use longer-term moving averages for more volatile stocks to reduce the chance that a meaningless price swing will trigger a stop-loss order to be executed.
- Adjust the moving averages to match target price ranges. For example, more extended targets should use broader moving averages to reduce the number of signals generated.
- Stop losses should not be closer than 1.5-times the current high-to-low range (volatility), as it is too likely to get executed without reason.
- Adjust the stop loss according to the market's volatility. If the stock price isn't moving too much, then the stop-loss points can be tightened.
- Use known significant events such as earnings releases, as crucial periods to be in or out of a trade as volatility and uncertainty can arise.

Calculating Expected Return

Setting stop-loss and take-profit points are also necessary to calculate the expected return. The importance of this calculation cannot be overstated, as it forces traders to think through their trades and rationalize them. As well, it gives them a systematic way to compare various trades and select only the most profitable ones.

This can be calculated using the following formula:

[(Probability of Gain) x (Take Profit % Gain)] + [(Probability of Loss) x (Stop-Loss % Loss)]

The result of this calculation is an expected return for the active trader, who will then measure it against other opportunities to determine which stocks to trade. The probability of gain or loss can be calculated by using true breakouts and breakdowns from the support or resistance levels — or for experienced traders, by making an educated guess.

Diversify and Hedge

Making sure you make the most of your trading means never putting your eggs in one basket. If you put all your money in one stock or one instrument, you're setting yourself up for a significant loss. So remember to diversify your investments - across both industry sector as well as market capitalization and geographic region. Not only does this help you manage your risk, but it also opens you up to more opportunities.

You may also find yourself a time when you need to hedge your position. Consider a stock position when the results are due. You may consider taking different place through options, which can help protect your position. When trading activity subsides, you can then unwind the hedge.

Downside Put Options

If you are approved for options trading, buying a downside put option, sometimes known as a protective put, can also be used as a hedge to stem losses from a trade that turns sour. A put option gives you the right, but not the obligation, to sell the underlying stock at a specified priced at or before the option expires. Therefore if you own XYZ stock from $100 and buy the 6-month $80 put for $1.00 per option in premium, then you will be effectively stopped out from any price drop below $79 ($80 strike minus the $1 premium paid).

The Bottom Line

Traders should always know when they plan to enter or exit a trade before they execute. By using stop losses effectively, a trader can minimize not only losses but also the number of times a trade is exited needlessly. In conclusion, make your battle plan ahead of time, so you'll already know you've won the war.

SECTION THREE

INTRODUCTION TO INFOMARKETING

For Infopreneurs, three tools help you retain customers in your subscription program. Here are some pointers on what those three tools are and how to use them.

Three tools should be integrated into an Info-Marketing business. Those are a utility, savings, and content and personality.

The utility is things that people build into their businesses. Things like the free or toll-free numbers that people call for more information. You teach people that strategy, and then you help them sign up with the actual provider. If they drop your continuity, then they lose the ability to use that system. Or you are providing it for them. So they sign up, they upgrade from one price to another, and they get all of that built for them. All they have to do is call in, and then you teach them how they can integrate it into their business.

The one thing that Jimmy V. and Travis Miller have is that they are providing a radio show ad. So if they go a month or two with those ads, and suddenly you drop out the program, the member will have to go figure out how you are going to get radio ads to replace the other things they were getting for their businesses. Whereas with newsletters, if you send three or four of those monthly newsletters out and you try not to send a fifth, you have customers calling you, "Hey, where's your newsletter?" While the newsletter is a tool they enjoy, radio commercials are integral to their business.

The good thing is, what you know, you usually teach the business owner, but you kind of boil it down and you give it to them on a website that they could sit an employee down for a day or two when the employee is just hired, and they learn the process. That will give you unlimited access to this staff-training program. Another excellent benefit to create is a training program for employers to help your customer get your training implemented. If I hire somebody, I want to be able to sit him or her down in front of that system. So that becomes part of the utility of my business. It becomes part of my employee-training program. And every time I hire a new employee, I have to have that program to help get the new employee accustomed to my business.

Next, are discounts. Savings and discounts can come in the form of exclusive access to vendors that they would not have access to otherwise or even know existed. So, let's say you tell somebody to implement a particular business strategy and they apply that and don't get the results you promised. A lot of times, they could file a lawsuit against you. Well, this is what that insurance will cover. Like my E & O policy is over $6,000 a year for the premium. Well, this is going to be $400 a year, because it is a group program for the association. I know not all of the IMA members have that type of coverage, but for the ones who do already, that is huge savings and more than justifies the price of being a member in the Information Marketing Association.

Personality is when people want to know what's going to happen next. Like how after the election, many people were wondering what did Rush say about the election? When Sarah Palin was nominated, what did Rush say about Sarah Palin? Everybody wants to know what they have to say about it. That is what you want to do within your business is, have people say, "I wonder what he thinks about that?" So they kind of tune in to hear what you have to say about it. It is these three principles that help make good businesses great and help to establish more buyers, more members, and more profit.

There have never been higher, more diverse, more lucrative opportunities for everyone-experienced, successful entrepreneurs to rank beginners-in the field of information marketing. If you can name a topic, there is a market for providing information about it. People buy information about almost everything-from hobbyist topics like dog training, to business topics like how to sell over the telephone, to self-improvement topics like fitness walking. The key is to find a responsive market and then package information that customers want in convenient forms such as DVD's, books, e-books, CD's, magazines, websites, teleseminars, webinars, coaching programs, seminars, and conferences.

REPLACING YOUR SALARY WITH INFORMARKETING INCOME WITHIN SIX MONTHS

What if you have no following, no fans, no list but want to create an information marketing business that supports you so you can retire or quit your job? And suppose you're eager to say sayonara to your paycheck within the next six months. Are there business models to follow that boost your chances of reaching that goal?

After giving this question a lot of thought, I've come up with five realistic strategies to generate a full-time income from selling information products and related services within six months.

1. Become an impresario. Remember Max Detweiler, the show producer who schemed to get the von

Trapp family singing on stage in The Sound of Music? An impresario today orchestrates events, which in the information marketing realm might be conferences, boot camps, web conference or virtual trade shows. To do this, you need a strong sense of what a definable, reachable audience wants to learn or experience along with a pleasant personality that can persuade well-known experts withdrawing power to participate in the events.

2. Become a product developer for others. Approach one or more people or companies that already have a strong following but few things for fans to buy. Offer to create their product empire in exchange for a percentage of the income. Start with merchandising ideas that can be implemented quickly, such as branded mugs, T-shirts and stickers and then proceed to the more expensive offerings, like group coaching programs, retreats, themed

tours and access to celebrities. You need both a high-flying imagination and practical marketing skills for this strategy.

3. Collect others' offerings in an online store. Identify a constituency that can't easily find a one-stop information hub with products to buy - such as left-handed musicians, parents of physically disabled children, nerdy women or aspiring crime scene analysts. Find courses, reports, consulting programs, etc. for this constituency that pays you a commission for each sale. Persuade additional people with general information products to create versions for your niche, with a commission for you. Use pay-per-click ads, media publicity, and joint ventures to generate traffic to your online store and resell buyers on related products and services after they become customers.

4. Aggressively develop your product line. To start with, select a niche and concentrate on product types for that niche that can be produced quickly, such as audio expert interviews or PDF compilations of advice. Within the first month, complete a free item, a low-cost item, a medium-priced offering, and a high-priced item and arrange them in a classic marketing funnel, where buyers at each level are encouraged to continue to the next level. Then use the traffic building techniques mentioned in strategy #3 to attract customers. And finally, continue to add to the product line as quickly as you can while maintaining product quality.

5. Use outsourcing to develop an assembly line of loosely related eBooks or DVDs. Here you are aiming at an existing marketplace that gathers millions of prospective buyers for you, such as Amazon's Kindle store (for eBooks) or Amazon and eBay (for DVDs).

Select a topic in which you have an avid interest and some knowledge. Use keyword research to identify product titles that are often searched for, and develop a cadre of trusted workers from sites like Fiverr, Guru or eLance who can create original work at low rates for which you purchase all rights. You serve the mastermind of this empire, with freelancers performing the content creation, quality control, cover creation, and marketing copy - unless you are already good at one or more of those tasks.

The above business models all aim at a speed of implementation for fast results. None is a lazy way to riches. Before getting started, calculate how much income you need to be clearing per month from your business to replace your salary, and when you have built to that level, you're ready to say goodbye to employment.

With an intelligent choice of topic and target market and a good measure of hard work, you should be able to accomplish your goal of exchanging the dependability of your job income for the freedom of the entrepreneurial life.

THE VITAL TOOLS FOR INFOMARKETING BUSINESS

Ask any info-marketer you know about his favorite online tools, and you're bound to have just opened a can of worms.

Colorful opinions of various types abound here. Not surprising, since Info Marketers rely on tools to create, maintain, and grow their online businesses. Like you'll never see a construction worker go to work without his tool belt…

…you'll never catch an info marketer leaving his home without his version of an "Info Marketing Toolkit" either. But with thousands of tools all over the web, how do you pick the right ones?

What are some of the critical tools an Info Marketer (or anyone) should have?

Let's find out.

Develop, Build, Market, Sell and Scale Using These Vital Tools

Tools help you create your online products. Tools are what help you sell them for years to come, too. Because various tools sometimes do similar things, info-marketers often choose a favorite.

For example, there are different kinds of membership plugins with different prices. Most do the same thing. Some prefer WordPress plugins, others prefer fully hosted solutions like Kajabi, and between these two, the options are vast.

The forms of content used to produce information products, as well as to market and house home websites around them, ranging from webinars, blogs, slides, video courses, email courses, marketing and much more.

Here is a list of highly recommended tools for your information marketing business.

Write Epic Ebooks With Penflip

Penflip makes writing ebooks or any long-form content easy. One of its highlight features is the way it lets you organize your writing by chapters within its main writing processor window. Focusing is made more comfortable with the minimalistic text editor that enables you to work on or offline. Just like the cloud-based Google Docs, the collaboration mode makes sharing feedback and editing possible. It also has a built-in revision history.

Once you're finished with your book, download your ebook with a single click. Your ebook can be downloaded into any format, including PDF, ePub, HTML, Mobi, and others.

Webinars: the Info Marketer's "Weapon of Mass Control?"

There are plenty of the usual suspects, but have you looked at omNovia?

Webinars are a versatile information marketing tool.

They can be recorded, packaged, and sold as information products or used as free valuable content for followers and customers. There are countless reasons to use webinars. To get the best quality, it's best to work with useful webinar tools. Here are some things to look out for:

- Easy for people to register and join.

- Up to date to 2015 standards.

- Support multiple joining options (phone, app).

- Ad-free and without a cap on attendees if you don't want one.

Other features to look for in webinar software is social integration, branding capabilities, data gather and analytics capabilities and one-click meeting recordings.

Here are a few excellent omNovia features:

- Twitter integration

- Interactive browser

- Slide show presenting

- AV remote

- Document sharing capabilities

- Instant webinar polls

- Record webinars

- Customize webinar interface

- Chat/Q&A options

- Hold slide show presentations

- Stream live webcasts in HD video

Another good option is GoToWebinar. It's been the info-marketers go-to for an unbroken string of years, and good reason. It's good software that works without problems. But is it up to date?

One gripe some have on GoToWebinar is that it doesn't have a "virtual waiting room" for people to standby in. If there is any downtime, a room like this serves as a communication channel to let people know what's going on rather than leave them in the dark.

Another reliable free option is Google Hangouts OnAir, but you can't record and sell webinars made with it.

Build Links & Create Epic Content with Text Editor Tool on Steroids: Zemanta

As an info marketer, you might or might not be an avid blogger. Chances are you at least have a blog that's kept up to date by you or an outsourcer.

Blog posts can be repackaged and used for information products. They have the power to provide free value to your current followers, gain new ones, and also rank you higher on Google thanks to the SEO juice good content offers.

Zemanta is a powerful plugin. It gives you content to use or refer to as you are writing in real-time. It's a text-editor plugin, a content creation tool, and it's also a link-building distribution tool.

Publishers can suggest content to other content creators who use Zemanta by paying a premium. This makes Zemanta an exceptional tool because, as a blogger, it kills two birds with one plugin. You get content inspiration and build links at the same time.

Craft Irresistible Headlines and Test Them To Perfection Using KingSumo Headlines

In case you haven't heard, headlines are arguably more important than the content pieces themselves.

Think that's absurd?

Here's an interesting statistic from the reputable Copyblogger about headlines:

"On average, 8 out of 10 people will read headline copy, but only 2 out of 10 will read the rest. This is the secret to the power of your title, and why it so highly determines the effectiveness of the entire piece."

If there is one thing you should be split testing, it's your headlines. And KingSumo can do this using a WordPress plugin

Of course, you need the traffic to use this plugin, but once you're getting some, plug this into your site and as you post you'll create separate headlines for each. This plugin will tell you the percentage of which gets the most impressions. It's a fool-proof way to optimize your blog posts.

Once you know the best headlines for your audience, your information products will automatically be more engaging and attractive as a result.

Gain New Customers By Giving Them Nothing But Value with LinkedIn's SlideShare

Slideshare is a content marketing tool that lets you distribute content through a new avenue using visual informational slides.

G2 Crowd describes SlideShares abilities here:

"SlideShare is the world's largest community for sharing presentations. With 60 million monthly visitors and 130 million page views, it is amongst the most visited 200 websites in the world. Besides presentations, SlideShare also supports documents, PDFs, videos, and webinars."

If you use decks to share content, SlideShare is perfect for your distribution. The premium version uploads presentations onto YouTube automatically.

SlideShare makes creating presentations easy, even if it's your weak point. Others are also able to collaborate online and pitch into the presentation creation. Information marketing can be dispersed in many ways, and today, SlideShare is one of the better ways to grow awareness around your professional messages.

Retarget Content & Provide More Value with Resonance

Resonance says on their website that 94.3% of site visitors will usually leave without a trace. That's why Resonance exists, to make sure you follow up with them.

Resonance is a retargeting content tool that focuses your content in front of the right eyes, those interested in your message. Track visitors and what they read on your website. Watch them stay longer as you use Resonance to provide them with more related content that they wouldn't know about without the retargeting.

The insights gained by retargeting data accumulated will help you formulate a bulletproof information product that is sure to be loved by its consumers.

Tools For Dominating With Social Media, Email And Automation

Information marketing often will rely on Social Media as a brand supporting platform. Because of this, a few social media tools are here to help the social media outreach strategies around your information products and marketing.

We'll start with a graphic design tool that enables anyone to make great visuals for any content or product they need, Canva.

Not a Graphic Designer? No Problem. Create Your Info Product and Blog Post Graphics With Canva

Canva makes all people professional designers.

Does the word Photoshop scare you?

Are you tired of outsourcing subpar graphics?

You need a Canva then.

Social Media is a very visual platform. I hope you're not posting articles without good quality-related images. Social media posts that use good photos get good results. Whether you're starting up or already have a large following, getting the perfect picture for each of your posts, do not have to be complicated.

Tip: The same image you use on your blog posts you can use on your social media posts. You might need to size things up differently, but for the most part, sharing images on social Media as previews to post isn't as strict for sizing as say a website hosted one.

Here's a general sizing guideline. Right-sized images get more social shares.

- Facebook: 1200×625

- LinkedIn: 800×800

- Pinterest: 735×1100

- Instagram: 1200×1200

- Google+: 800×1200

- Twitter: 1024×510

Canva is perfect for images if you're not a natural-born graphic designer and haven't taken the time to learn the skills, yet still want to take a crack at doing your images.

Everyone uses the same free stock photos. They often look good, but after seeing it again and again, it serves as a negative thing instead of an image that will draw engagement.

Create fresh, eye-popping images that force people to click using Canva. Canva gives you template options that zone in on select social media channels. The sizing is listed above for your information, but with Canva, you will not need to know to size for individual platforms to get the most shares for your posts. Canva does it for you. Just select the template where it's going under the "Layouts" tab, and you're good to go.

Every info marketer, regardless of graphics skills, should have Canva in their toolkits.

Never Be Out Of The Loop With Tagboard

By knowing which brands are saying what about who, you gain leveraging power in your industry. By capitalizing every chance you get to engage with your followers, you fortify your info marketing business with this successful social media mindset.

Tagboard makes sure you never ignore a follower or a mention of your brand.

It lists for you the latest posts on various social networks like Instagram and Twitter that use any select hashtag term you specify for in the Tagboard Search Bar.

Gain insights on what your customers are searching for

- Monitor non-brand keywords
- Follow people interested in select hashtags
- Interact with people involved in preferred hashtags

Quickly monitor your brand keywords with ease and daily to never skip a beat.

Find High-Quality Leads On Twitter With Socedo

In case you didn't know it possible, it is entirely doable now to locate and qualify leads from Twitter thanks to Socedo. With Socedo, all that needs to be done is a quick keyword search to generate a valuable list full of targeted prospects. Let me list out more benefits Socedo provides:

- Automatically favorite tweets
- Automatically follow opportunities
- Automatically send direct messages
- Fine-tune custom criteria with provided business insights

Get Started With Marketing Automation

Marketing Automation, according to Hubspot, is a type of software that allows people to:

"Nurture prospects with highly personalized, useful content that helps convert prospects to customers and turn customers into delighted customers."

With marketing automation, you can revolutionize the way you do your email marketing. Forget about lists. Forget about double entries in multiple lists. Marketing automation allows you to tag people based on interest; therefore, quickly searching for the right subscribers for future promotions becomes a breeze.

The nightmare of multiple list management suddenly becomes a lot less scary with automation marketing. You won't want to get too deep into marketing automation until you have fresh new organic leads coming to you regularly. The same Hubspot article explains why:

"Too many marketers without inbound lead generation strategies spend their time figuring out how to take the tiny fraction of the market they already have in their database as leads and squeeze more out of them."

Tip: Use Drip to place a JavaScript snippet on the footer of each of your pages and then capture leads from each of those pages with it.

Get Personal With AutoSend

Engaging customers, followers, readers, and clients is a vital focus for information marketers and service providers alike.

As an info product creator, chances are you grow your email list. With AutoSend, you make subscribing a much more personal thing.

You can 10x your engagement with these AutoSend features:

- Automatically send personalized email or SMS to each new customer solely based on their actions on your site (the result is an extremely targeted message)
- Send a personal message even if that person just visited your About Me or FAQ page.
- Convert more visitors into longtime, paying customers that bring others just like them to your subscription-based business.

Wrapping It Up: Dedicated Action + Tools = Winning

The truth is that Information Product Marketing requires dedicated action – and the right tools.

Use these tools to keep your action optimized for peak return on time and effort and money investments put into it.

Make sure your content production is prime, your social media outreach is consistent and engaging, and that your email marketing is set up to generate interaction and grow conversions.

Information marketing has been around since pre-internet days, but thanks to tools like these, the internet is now the ultimate info product selling platform.

Drip is an Email Service Provider that makes automation marketing attainable for even beginner info-marketers.

www.ingramcontent.com/pod-product-compliance
Lightning Source LLC
Chambersburg PA
CBHW030652220526
45463CB00005B/1746